Half-light

Yevgeny Baratynsky
Half-light
AND OTHER POEMS

Translated and introduced by
PETER FRANCE

PUBLICATIONS
2015

Published by Arc Publications,
Nanholme Mill, Shaw Wood Road
Todmorden OL14 6DA, UK
www.arcpublications.co.uk

Translation copyright © Peter France 2015
Copyright in Introduction © Peter France 2015
Copyright in the present edition © Arc Publications 2015

978 1908376 88 6 (pbk)
978 1908376 89 3 (hbk)
978 1908376 90 9 (ebk)

Design by Tony Ward
Cover design by Tony Ward
Printed by Lightning Source

ACKNOWLEDGEMENTS

There are one or more variant versions for many of the poems
printed here. With a small number of exceptions on points of
detail (notably in the poem 'Rhyme'), the translations have
been made from the one-volume edition of Baratynsky's
poems edited by L. G. Frizman and published in the *Novaya
Biblioteka Poeta* collection (St Petersburg, 2000). Earlier versions
of some of the translations appeared in *Fulcrum, Cardinal
Points, International Literary Quarterly, The Penguin Book of
Russian Poetry* (ed. R. Chandler, 2015) and *European Romantic
Poetry* (ed. M. Ferber, 2005). The translator's thanks go to all
those who have helped and encouraged him in this labour of
love, in particular Robert Chandler, Boris Dralyuk, Ilya Kutik,
Irina Mashinski, Siân Reynolds and Antony Wood.

'Arc Classics:
New Translations of Great Poets of the Past'
Series Editor: Jean Boase-Beier

*To the memory of my dear friend
and co-translator,
the poet Jon Stallworthy*

CONTENTS

Introduction / 9

OTHER POEMS

Among the great figures of Russian literature, Yevgeny Baratynsky is one of the least known outside Russia. Why this should be so is rather mysterious. Partly it must be due to the 'purgatory' that he suffered for some sixty years after his death in 1844 – and again in post-Revolutionary Russia, where it was only in the last third of the twentieth century that he came into his own as one of the outstanding poets in the language.

Whatever the cause, for the most part he has been published in English in a fragmentary way. And yet there is a lot that might attract foreign readers to his poetry. Of all European writers of the time, he seems closest to Giacomo Leopardi, long considered one of Italy's greatest lyric poets. Leopardi, born in 1798 and dying in 1837, was an almost exact contemporary of Baratynsky (1800-1844), and there is much in the clear-sighted, bleak vision of man and society in the *Canti* that reminds one of the poet of *Half-light*: the historical pessimism, the *noia* (something like Baudelaire's *spleen*), the awareness of human fragility and ephemerality, but also the idealism and the vital honesty and magnanimity.

The parallels are not exact of course. Leopardi's poetic language, with its unprecedented exploration of freer verse forms, is quite different from that of the classicist Baratynsky, for whom metre and (usually) rhyme gave strength and permanence to poetry. And although both came from noble families that were removed from real power, Leopardi's situation in post-Napoleonic Italy was poles apart from the Russian poet's experience of post-Napoleonic Russia. Their private lives, too, though both difficult, evolved in quite separate ways.

Yevgeny Abramovich Baratynsky (sometimes spelled Boratynsky) was born in the first year of the new century on the family property in the Tambov region of central Russia. His father, losing the favour of Tsar Paul I, went to live in the country, devoting himself to improving his estate and creating a beautiful garden. Yevgeny remembered this garden fondly (see the poem 'Enchanted Groves' on pp. 104-7 below), but he was less influenced by his father than by his strong-willed, intelligent and affectionate mother, Aleksandra Fyodorovna Cherepanova (many of his letters to her survive and some have been translated into English by G. R. Barratt [The Hague, 1973]). The boy was at first educated by tutors at home, but after his father's death in 1810, he was given a place at the School of Pages, an elite boarding school in St Petersburg. To all appearances, his future was assured.

His school days, in which he discovered a love for literature and the desire to be a poet, were cut short by an event that changed the course of his life. Whether in emulation of the Robin-Hood activities of the hero of Schiller's *Die Räuber* (as he later claimed) or simply to buy good things for his sixteenth birthday party, he and a classmate stole a substantial sum of money from another classmate's father; they were immediately found out, disgraced and expelled from the school. A career as an officer was now closed to Baratynsky, especially in view of the personal disfavour of the tsar. Even so, after a period of suicidal depression, he decided to attempt to rehabilitate himself by enlisting as a private soldier.

His conditions of service were in fact quite favourable. At first he continued to live in St Petersburg, where he was one of a circle of highly gifted poets (later to be considered as the Pléiade of the Golden Age), including Aleksandr Pushkin, for many years a friend and ally, and his particular friend Anton Delvig. Before long he was transferred to Finland, but even here he was able to make frequent visits to St Petersburg – unlike Pushkin, who was at the same time exiled to the distant South for four years. Baratynsky's view of Finland was a Romantic one, full of granite cliffs and waterfalls – his affecting long poem, 'Eda', set among Finnish country people, is a northern equivalent of Pushkin's verse tale of the tragic love of a Russian soldier and a village girl, 'The Prisoner of the Caucasus'

– and Pushkin thought highly of his rival's poem. The years spent in Finland were in fact very productive of verse, much of it published, sometimes with cuts imposed by the censor, in advanced St Petersburg journals. At this time Baratynsky was close to the young writers and officers who embraced the Decembrist cause, yet he himself, though he sympathised with their radical ideas and aspirations, held back for the most part from direct political commitment, as some of the Decembrists noted in their unfavourable reactions to 'Eda'.

In May 1825, after nine years of disgrace, and just a few months before the ill-fated December uprising against the newly crowned tsar Nicholas I, Baratynsky was finally pardoned and promoted to officer rank. At the end of the same year, he retired from the service and moved to Moscow to be near his ailing mother. The following year he married Nastasya L'vovna Engel'gardt, and for nearly twenty years the couple lived principally in Moscow or in nearby Muranovo, an estate belonging to Baratynsky's wife. The marriage was a happy one, but this was a difficult period for Baratynsky, particularly the years between 1833 and 1842. In Moscow, then rather a provincial city, he was far from the centre of the literary world; he wrote to a friend in 1825: 'The fate I can anticipate will be like the monotonous Russian plains, covered in snow as they are now, and presenting an eternally melancholy prospect.' Worse than this, in the wake of the failed Decembrist coup Russia was in the grip of despotic rule and political repression, and the general feeling of hopelessness naturally communicated itself to a sensitive and idealistic spirit such as Baratynsky. In addition, he found himself uncomfortably torn between the two ideological camps that struggled over Russia's future, the Slavophils and the Westernizers. At the end of the 1830s he wrote to another correspondent: 'These last ten years of existence, which seem at first glance to have nothing special about them, have been for me more burdensome than all my years of confinement in Finland.'

But they were also productive years, the years of his best poetry. He found new literary allies, and a new inspiration in the work of German philosophers. His first volume of poetry was published in 1827, followed by a much larger collection in 1835 – the latter in two volumes, the first devoted to short poems, the second to longer ones such as 'Eda' and the satirical, yet elegiac 'Feasts'. Then in 1842 came *Half-light*, Baratynsky's most important work, a gathering of poems written since 1834 and presented as a unified whole under a highly meaningful title. By the time of its publication, however, the poets of the Golden Age had largely gone out of fashion, and Baratynsky with them; many reactions to his new book were negative or indifferent.

The same year of 1842 saw an imperial decree which seemed to promise a reform, or even an end, of serfdom; timid and abortive though this was, it was greeted at first with enthusiasm. The general atmosphere became more hopeful, and Baratynsky shared in this positive mood. In 1843 he set out on his first visit to Western Europe, spending the winter in Paris, where he discussed politics with friends of the radical thinker Aleksandr Herzen – but also read his poems in his own French prose translation in literary gatherings, where they apparently contributed to the birth of the French 'poème en prose'. Looking back after his death on Baratynsky's mood at this time, a Paris-based Russian poet wrote:

He looked on life with melancholy but boldly
and was always pressing onwards;
he thirsted for activity, and called on us to act...

From Paris he travelled to Italy, and some of his poems of this time breathe a striking new air of hope, notably 'Steamship', one of his last poems, written during a sea journey, where he seems to celebrate the collaboration of nature and modern human activity.

'Steamship' ends with the line: 'Tomorrow I see Elysium on earth'. It seemed as if Italy was exercising its customary magic. But read with hindsight, this final poem takes on a different coloration, for a few weeks after Baratynsky's arrival in Italy he died, quite unexpectedly. His body was brought back by sea and buried in St Petersburg. Only a few friends came to the funeral, notably Prince Vyazemsky, one of the last survivors of the Golden Age and the addressee of Baratynsky's dedication of *Half-light*. And with his death a twilight set in for his reputation, an obscurity that lasted until the Symbolists brought a new dawn at the beginning of the new century.

'It is high time that Baratynsky finally got the place on the Russian Parnassus that has long belonged to him'. Such was Pushkin's wish, and Victor Terras's *Handbook of Russian Literature* notes that today his wish has come true in Russia, but that 'Baratynsky is still little known outside Russia'. That was written in the 1980s, but as far as the English-speaking world is concerned, things haven't changed a great deal. *Half-light* has never been published in English translation. True, there are translations of a number of poems in various anthologies, including those of Alan Myers in his selection of nineteenth-century Russian poetry, *An Age Ago* (Farrar, Straus and Giroux, 1988, with a foreword by Joseph Brodsky). Five poems from *Half-light* also appear in what seems to be the only volume devoted solely to Baratynsky in English, the *Selected Poems* by Jill Higgs (Hub Editions, Spalding, 2004).

Half-light (Сумерки), which is given here in its entirety,

As this volume goes to press, a new and substantial translation of Baratynsky's poems and essays by Rawley Grau is announced from Ugly Duckling Presse, New York, under the title *A Science not for the Earth*. Clearly, Baratynsky's moment has arrived for the English-speaking world.

13

seems to me the best introduction to Baratynsky's verse, containing a full range of his different forms (except for narrative verse) and styles. As noted above, he presented it as a coherent book of lyric verse – a novelty in Russia in 1842. The title, which might also be translated as 'Twilight' or 'Dusk' (though the Russian word could also refer to the period before dawn) can be read as a reference to the poet's own position, forgotten and out of fashion. Equally, it evokes the state of Russian poetry after the setting of its sun (Pushkin's death in a duel, which is alluded to indirectly in the closing stanzas of 'Autumn', itself a response to Pushkin's poem of the same name), and more generally the gloomy situation of Russia under the repressive rule of Nicholas I. This central collection is followed here by a selection of Baratynsky's other poems; most of these come from the period 1822-1833, but the last two are from the last years of his life.

Jill Higgs's volume of translations from Baratynsky carries this declaration of intention: 'to follow the metrical and rhyme schemes as closely as possible, believing that a poet's message resides in the sound and cadence of his verse as well as in the individual words.' It's impossible not to agree with a belief in the significance of sound in poetry (as indeed in all writing), but one can question whether it need oblige one to imitate as faithfully as possible the prosody of the original – as Brodsky famously believed was the duty of the translator of poetry. Metre and rhyme have a specific function within a given poetic tradition that may well not translate into a different culture – witness the fate of the Homeric hexameter in English. It's a pity that so many theorists of translation, from Schleiermacher to Nabokov or Brodsky, have felt the need – sometimes in defence of their own practice – to proclaim the one true method of translation.

The translations offered here are 'close' rather than 'free'. I have tried to convey the details of Baratynsky's meaning, the meaning his poems had for his contemporaries. But I haven't attempted a period rendering, either in vocabulary or in syntax; I have avoided poetic inversions, for instance, and the constructions and expressions used here all seem to me to be readily usable in our own time, though they may in some cases also belong to Baratynsky's British contemporaries. I don't, of course, follow Baratynsky word for word, nor indeed line for line, though there are generally the same number of lines here as in the originals. In some cases, the metre is close to that of the original, even if the alternation of masculine and feminine endings is sometimes sacrificed. Elsewhere, the prosody has been changed, though never drastically and always with the intention of producing the same kind of effect – I have tried to echo what I hear (subjectively, no doubt) as the poet's voice rather than the precise form that embodies it. For instance, the alternation of rhymed 'strophe' and unrhymed 'antistrophe' in 'The Last Poet' is mine rather than Baratynsky's; he sets the rhymed iambic pentameters of the odd stanzas against the equally rhymed trochaic tetrameters of the even ones.

In all cases, though, I have aimed for a definite, if sometimes irregularly executed, metrical structure; this seems to me an essential constituent in the poised clarity which 'contains' Baratynsky's disturbing vision. Rhyme is more problematic; its importance for Baratynsky is evident in the poem he devotes to it (rhyme as a consolation for lost harmony), and all the poems of Half-light, with the exception of three short hexameter pieces, are fully rhymed. Like almost all translators of poetry today, I baulk at the idea of reflecting all the regular rhymes of the Russian, but have aimed to preserve the rhyming principle with a variety of slant rhymes, alliterations, assonances and the like.

Baratynsky occupies a special place in Russian literature, and I think he may be an acquired taste – I have certainly grown increasingly attached to his writing as I have translated

15

it over the years. He was a contemporary of the Romantics, and one whose characteristic themes are typical of the period, but who avoided the self-indulgence of much Romanticism, looking back rather to the strong impersonality of the eighteenth-century ode. The poems of *Half-light* are of different kinds, from a playful compaint in unrhymed hexameters to a troublesome fly ('A Grumble') to the elaborate stanzas of the classical odes 'To Autumn' and 'The Last Poet'. Only rarely do they respond openly to particular situations – virtually no annotation is needed. They are lyrics which express, directly or indirectly, personal reactions, emotions, and ideas, but the tone is frequently impersonal, and the poems confront profound issues of human psychology and historical destiny, often contrasting nineteenth-century scientific rationalism with the lost wholeness of an earlier world.

Pushkin famously said of Baratynsky: 'He is an exception among us, because he thinks', and this has given rise to the standard view of Baratynsky as a 'philosopher poet'. He thought, of course, as did Pushkin and all his contemporaries, but he was not a devotee of 'sovereign reason'. On the contrary, as a poem like 'Thought, yet more thought' makes painfully clear, he saw rational thinking as a curse rather than an achievement. The reader does well to bear in mind the words of one of his most eloquent modern champions, the poet and critic Ilya Kutik: 'As a poet Baratynsky was neither a philosopher nor a thinker. He was a fearless, dispassionate spectator of himself and his actions, seen in an epic light.'

Peter France

СУМЕРКИ

❧

HALF-LIGHT

КНЯЗЮ ПЕТРУ АНДРЕЕВИЧУ ВЯЗЕМСКОМУ

Как жизни общие призывы,
Как увлеченья суеты,
Понятны вам страстей порывы
И обаяния мечты;
Понятны вам все дуновенья,
Которым в море бытия
Послушна наша ладия.
Вам приношу я песнопенья,
Где отразилась жизнь моя,
Исполнена тоски глубокой,
Противоречий, слепоты,
И между тем любви высокой,
Любви добра и красоты.

Счастливый сын уединенья,
Где сердца ветреные сны
И мысли праздные стремленья
Разумно мной усыплены;
Где, другу мира и свободы,
Ни до фортуны, ни до моды,
Ни до молвы мне нужды нет;
Где я простил безумству, злобе
И позабыл, как бы во гробе,
Но добровольно, шумный свет, –
Еще порою покидаю
Я Лету, созданную мной,
И степи мира облетаю
С тоскою жаркой и живой.
Ищу я вас; гляжу: что с вами?
Куда вы брошены судьбами,
Вы, озарявшие меня
И дружбы кроткими лучами
И светом высшего огня?
Что вам дарует провиденье?
Чем испытует небо вас?

TO PRINCE PYOTR ANDREEVICH VYAZEMSKY

You know not just the calls to action
and the petty frets that fill our days,
but equally the surge of passion,
and all the blandishments of dream;
you understand the wayward winds
that on the ocean of existence
can beach our vessel on the sands.
To you I give this book of verses –
it bears the imprint of my life,
filled as it is with melancholy,
blind compulsions and inward strife,
but also with an exalted love
for all that is beautiful and good.

The happy child of solitude,
where with the soothing voice of reason
I calm the heart's unsteady dreams
and the mind's idle agitation;
where, as a friend of peace and freedom,
I have no time for wealth and fame;
where I forgive unreason, anger,
and willingly, a distant stranger,
forget the world's discordant games, –
I still from time to time abandon
the Lethe I have made, and I
fly over the world's barren garden
with burning longing and desire.
I search for you, to know your fortune:
where can destiny have brought you,
you who once lit my youthful way
with friendship's unassuming candle
and with a high poetic flame?
What gifts has providence reserved you?
How has heaven tried your heart?

И возношу молящий глас:
Да длится ваше упоенье,
Да скоро минет скорбный час!

Звезда разрозненной плеяды!
Так из глуши моей стремлю
Я к вам заботливые взгляды,
Вам высшей благости молю,
От вас отвлечь судьбы суровой
Удары грозные хочу,
Хотя вам прозою почтовой
Лениво дань мою плачу.

I raise my voice in supplication:
Long may your inward fire burn brightly!
Soon may your grieving time be past!

Star of our scattered constellation!
Out from my hermitage I gaze
with anxious, fond anticipation,
and wish you bright, unclouded days,
and pray kind heaven to protect you
from the savage blows of sullen fate,
though when it comes to writing letters,
I lazily procrastinate.

The poet Pyotr Andreevich Vyazemsky (1792-1878) was a member of an ancient noble family and a leading figure in the culture of Russia's 'Golden Age'.

ПОСЛЕДНИЙ ПОЭТ

Век шествует путем своим железным,
В сердцах корысть, и общая мечта
Час от часу насущным и полезным
Отчетливей, бесстыдней занята.
Исчезнули при свете просвещенья
Поэзии ребяческие сны,
И не о ней хлопочут поколенья,
Промышленным заботам преданы.

Для ликующей свободы
Вновь Эллада ожила,
Собрала свои народы
И столицы подняла;
В ней опять цветут науки,
Носит понт торговли груз,
Но не слышны лиры звуки
В первобытном рае муз!

Блестит зима дряхлеющего мира,
Блестит! Суров и бледен человек;
Но зелены в отечестве Омира
Холмы, леса, брега лазурных рек.
Цветет Парнас! пред ним, как в оны годы,
Кастальский ключ живой струею бьет;
Нежданный сын последних сил природы –
Возник Поэт: идет он и поет.

Воспевает, простодушный,
Он любовь и красоту
И науки, им ослушной,
Пустоту и суету:
Мимолетные страданья
Легкомыслием целя,
Лучше, смертный, в дни незнанья
Радость чувствует земля.

THE LAST POET

It strides along its iron track, our century:
the people's dream, as hearts succumb to greed,
with every hour more clearly, shamelessly
is swallowed in utility and need.
Enlightenment with her clarity dispels
the childish dreams by which the poet lives,
and generations, thirsting after wealth,
care nothing for the gifts the poet gives.

> Hellas has sprung again,
> jubilant in her freedom,
> gathers her people together,
> raises up cities;
> knowledge flowers afresh,
> rich cargoes ride the Aegean,
> but the lyre lies low, unheard
> in the paradise of the muses.

It shines, the winter of the decrepit world –
it shines! Humanity looks pale and grim,
but in the land of Homer green is unfurled
on hills and woods and banks of azure streams.
Parnassus flowers; as once upon a time,
Castalia's water gushes at its base;
unlooked-for son of nature in decline,
the poet has risen – and lifts up his voice.

> Simple-hearted he sings
> songs of love and of beauty,
> sings how science scorns them
> in her empty fretting:
> with insouciance healing
> ephemeral suffering,
> earth knows joy more fully
> in the days of unknowing.

23

Поклонникам Урании холодной
Поет, увы! он благодать страстей;
Как пажити Эол бурнопогодный,
Плодотворят они сердца людей;
Живительным дыханием развита,
Фантазия подъемлется от них,
Как некогда возникла Афродита
Из пенистой пучины вод морских.

И зачем не предадимся
Снам улыбчивым своим?
Бодрым сердцем покоримся
Думам робким, а не им!
Верьте сладким убежденьям
Вас ласкающих очес
И отрадным откровеньям
Сострадательных небес!

Суровый смех ему ответом; персты
Он на струнах своих остановил,
Сомкнул уста вещать полуотверсты,
Но гордыя главы не преклонил:
Стопы свои он в мыслях направляет
В немую глушь, в безлюдный край; но свет
Уж праздного вертепа не являет,
И на земле уединенья нет!

Человеку непокорно
Море синее одно,
И свободно, и просторно,
И приветливо оно;
И лица не изменило
С дня, в который Аполлон
Поднял вечное светило
В первый раз на небосклон.

To chilly-hearted Urania's worshippers
he sings, alas! of passion's gifts to art:
as winter tempests fertilize the earth,
passion brings plenty to the human heart.
Engendered and nurtured by its living breath,
fancy takes wing and soars, as once above
the ocean's foaming depths that raged beneath
rose Aphrodite, bringing love.

> Why not give ourselves over
> to our smiling dreams?
> Yet with cheerful hearts
> we think craven thoughts!
> Trust the sweet urgings
> of eyes that caress you
> and the bright revelations
> of compassionate heaven!

A stony laugh replied, he checked the motion
of fingers as they strayed across the lyre,
closed tight the lips that prophecy had opened,
but still he proudly keeps his head held high;
and in the world of thought he makes his way
to the dumb wilderness, the desert heath –
but there is now no cave where he can lay
his head, no room for solitude on earth.

> The blue sea alone
> resists man's will;
> spacious and free,
> it bids us welcome;
> and its face is the same
> since the day when Apollo
> first raised his undying
> flame in the firmament.

Оно шумит перед скалой Левкада.
На ней певец, мятежной думы полн,
Стоит… в очах блеснула вдруг отрада:
Сия скала… тень Сафо!… песни волн…
Где погребла любовница Фаона
Отверженной любви несчастный жар,
Там погребет питомец Аполлона
Свои мечты, свой бесполезный дар!

И по-прежнему блистает
Хладной роскошию свет;
Серебрит и позлащает
Свой безжизненный скелет;
Но в смущение приводит
Человека вал морской,
И от шумных вод отходит
Он с тоскующей душой!

It roars beneath Leucadia's rocky heights.
The bard stands there, deep in tumultuous thought,
he stands... and suddenly joy fills his eyes:
this rock... and Sappho's shade... the waves' uproar...
Where spurned by Phaon once the lovesick poet
buried in ocean her unhappiness,
there too will he, Apollo's favourite,
bury his useless gifts, his hopeless dreams!

As of old the world gleams,
luxuriant and frigid,
silver and gilt
on lifeless bones;
but the crashing sea
dismays the poet,
and with desolate soul
he quits the loud waves!

* * *

Предрассудок! он обломок
Давней правды. Храм упал;
А руин его потомок
Языка не разгадал.

Гонит в нем наш век надменный,
Не узнав его лица,
Нашей правды современной
Дряхлолетнего отца.

Воздержи младую силу!
Дней его не возмущай;
Но пристойную могилу,
Как уснет он, предку дай.

* * *

Prejudice? just a fragment
of ancient truth. The temple is gone;
those who remain cannot unravel
the words that speak to them from its ruin.

Unable to recognize his features,
our haughty century disdains
the old, decrepit ancestor
of what we call the truth today.

Restrain your youthful energy!
Do not distress his final days;
but raise an honourable grave
to your forefather's memory.

НОВИНСКОЕ
А. С. Пушкину

Она улыбкою своей
Поэта в жертвы пригласила,
Но не любовь ответом ей
Взор ясный думой осенила.
Нет, это был сей легкий сон,
Сей тонкий сон воображенья,
Что посылает Аполлон
Не для любви – для вдохновенья.

NOVINSKOE

to A. S. Pushkin

That day she tempted with a smile
the poet to her pliant court,
but love was not the cloud that fell
on his clear brow in passing thought.
No, it was the ethereal dream
of exquisite imagination,
the dream Apollo sends to feed
not love, but inspiration.

Novinskoe was a village outside Moscow, a favourite place for fash-
ionable excursions, visited by Pushkin after his return from exile.

ПРИМЕТЫ

Пока человек естества не пытал
　　Горнилом, весами и мерой,
Но детски вещаньям природы внимал,
　　Ловил ее знаменья с верой;

Покуда природу любил он, она
　　Любовью ему отвечала,
О нем дружелюбной заботы полна,
　　Язык для него обретала.

Почуя беду над его головой,
　　Вран каркал ему в опасенье,
И замысла, в пору смирясь пред судьбой,
　　Воздерживал он дерзновенье.

На путь ему выбежав из лесу волк,
　　Крутясь и подъемля щетину,
Победу пророчил, и смело свой полк
　　Бросал он на вражью дружину.

Чета голубиная, вея над ним,
　　Блаженство любви прорицала.
В пустыне безлюдной он не был одним:
　　Нечуждая жизнь в ней дышала.

Но, чувство презрев, он доверил уму;
　　Вдался в суету изысканий…
И сердце природы закрылось ему,
　　И нет на земле прорицаний.

SIGNS

Before humanity put nature to the test
    with scales and crucibles and measures,
while we still listened child-like to her voice,
    the ear of faith received her treasures;

as long as man loved nature, she repaid
    his love, and seeing in mankind
a friend and brother, her affection made
    a language he could understand.

Sensing disaster hanging overhead,
    the raven croaked a warning,
and he, submitting to the will of fate,
    abandoned his rash undertaking.

Or else a wolf leapt out upon his path,
    twisting and turning, bristling fur,
a sign of victory – and he led his men
    out to the battle without fear.

A pair of pigeons fluttering over him
    foretold the blessedness of love.
In unpeopled deserts he was not alone,
    surrounded by familiar life.

But he scorned feeling, put his trust in thought,
    absorbed himself in vain research...
He lost the key to nature's heart,
    and prophecy is dead on earth.

* * *

Всегда и в пурпуре и в злате,
В красе негаснущих страстей,
Ты не вздыхаешь об утрате
Какой-то младости твоей.
И юных граций ты прелестней!
И твой закат пышней, чем день!
Ты сладострастней, ты телесней
Живых, блистательная тень!

* * *

Увы! Творец непервых сил!
На двух статейках утомил
Ты кой-какое дарованье!
Лишенный творческой мечты,
Уже, в жару нездравом, ты
Коверкать стал правописанье!

Неаполь возмутил рыбарь,
И, власть прияв, как мудрый царь,
Двенадцать дней он градом правил;
Но что же? – непривычный ум,
Устав от венценосных дум,
Его в тринадцатый оставил.

* * *

Always in purple and in gold,
in deathless passion's beauty clad,
you do not mourn the days of old,
the loss of what they call your youth.
More beautiful than youthful graces,
your sunset is richer than bright day.
You are voluptuous and carnal
more than the living, brilliant shade!

* * *

Alas! poor average writer, how
two little sketches have worn out
gifts that are hardly worth the shilling!
Empty of all creative fire,
with sickly warmth you now conspire
to tinker with the rules of spelling!

A Naples fisherman, they say,
rebelled, took power and for twelve days
like a wise monarch ruled the province.
But what came next? His mind, not used
to rule, on day thirteen refused
and marched him back to his poor hovel.

НЕДОНОСОК

Я из племени духов,
Но не житель Эмпирея,
И, едва до облаков
Возлетев, паду, слабея.
Как мне быть? Я мал и плох;
Знаю: рай за их волнами,
И ношусь, крылатый вздох,
Меж землей и небесами.

Блещет солнце – радость мне!
С животворными лучами
Я играю в вышине
И веселыми крылами
Ластюсь к ним, как облачко;
Пью счастливо воздух тонкой,
Мне свободно, мне легко,
И пою я птицей звонкой.

Но ненастье заревет
И до облак, свод небесный
Омрачивших, вознесет
Прах земной и лист древесный:
Бедный дух! ничтожный дух!
Дуновенье роковое
Вьет, крутит меня, как пух,
Мчит под небо громовое.

Бури грохот, бури свист!
Вихорь хладный! вихорь жгучий!
Бьет меня древесный лист,
Удушает прах летучий!
Обращусь ли к небесам,
Оглянуся ли на землю –
Грозно, черно тут и там;
Вопль унылый я подъемлю.

STILLBORN

I am one of the spirit tribe,
yet the sky is not my dwelling;
hardly have I reached the clouds
than I fall back, weakly flailing.
What can I do, so small and weak?
I know paradise is hidden
beyond them and like a winged sigh
I float between earth and heaven.

The radiant sun is my joy.
I play in its life-giving light
high up in the lofty sky
on joyous wings and in flight
I cling to its rays like a cloud,
drinking the subtle air,
light as dust, free as the wind,
a bird's voice loud and clear.

But the tempest roars and sweeps
dust of earth and leaves of trees
up to the clouds that spread
darkness on radiant skies,
poor spirit of nothingness!
The fateful winds now rend
and hurl me like a speck of dust
from the storm-racked firmament.

Thunder and whistling of storms!
Whirlwind that chills and burns!
My head battered by flying leaves,
I choke in the dust that swirls.
I can turn my eyes to heaven
or look to the earth below –
up or down, all is black and grim,
I raise a desperate howl.

Смутно слышу я порой
Клич враждующих народов,
Поселян беспечных вой
Под грозой их переходов,
Гром войны и крик страстей,
Плач недужного младенца...
Слезы льются из очей:
Жаль земного поселенца!

Изнывающий тоской,
Я мечусь в полях небесных,
Надо мной и подо мной
Беспредельных – скорби тесных!
В тучу прячусь я, и в ней
Мчуся, чужд земного края,
Страшный глас людских скорбей
Гласом бури заглушая.

Мир я вижу как во мгле;
Арф небесных отголосок
Слабо слышу... На земле
Оживил я недоносок.
Отбыл он без бытия:
Роковая скоротечность!
В тягость роскошь мне твоя,
О бессмысленная вечность!

Dimly at times I hear
the din of enemy tribes,
shrieks of uncaring hordes,
turbulent, frenzied, wild,
war's thunder, the passions' voice,
weeping of the sick child...
and tears stream down my face –
pity for the sad world.

Sorrow gnaws at my breast,
I fling through the plains of air
wide above and below my head –
yet too narrow to house my care!
I hide in the clouds to flee
the strange world, I try to drown
the terrible human cries
of woe in the howl of the storm.

I see the world as through a haze,
dimly hear the harps that play
in heaven... I brought to life
a thing stillborn, it ebbed away –
never knew what it is to be:
bleak ephemerality!
Your wealth lies heavy on me,
senseless eternity!

АЛКИВИАД

Облокотясь перед медью, образ его отражавшей,
Дланью слегка приподняв кудри златые чела,
Юный красавец сидел, горделиво-задумчив, и, смехом
Горьким смеясь, на него мужи казали перстом;
Девы, тайно любуясь челом благородно-открытым,
Нехотя взор отводя, хмурили брови свои.
Он же глух был и слеп; он, не в меди глядясь, а в грядущем,
Думал: к лицу ли ему будет лавровый венок?

РОПОТ

Красного лета отрава, муха досадная, что ты
Вьешься, терзая меня, льнешь то к лицу, то к перстам?
Кто одарил тебя жалом, властным прервать самовольно
Мощно-крылатую мысль, жаркой любви поцелуй?
Ты из мечтателя мирного, нег европейских питомца,
Дикого скифа творишь, жадного смерти врага.

ALCIBIADES

Propped on his elbows in front of the bronze that reflected him,
one hand lightly lifting the golden curls from his brow,
the beautiful youth was sitting in haughty thought, while the men
pointed their fingers at him, laughing a bitter laugh;
admiring in secret his noble wide forehead, the maidens
unwillingly turned their eyes away, and frowned,
but he was deaf and blind, gazing not at the bronze but the future,
and thought: would a wreath of laurel become that brow?

A GRUMBLE

Bane of the gorgeous summer, meddlesome fly, why must you
torture me, ducking and weaving, clinging to face and to fingers?
Who was it gave you that sting that has power to cut short at will
thought on its albatross wings or the burning kisses of love?
You make of the peaceable thinker, bred on the pleasures of Europe,
a barbarous Scythian warrior, thirsting for enemy blood.

МУДРЕЦУ

Тщетно меж бурною жизнью и хладною смертью, философ,
Хочешь ты пристань найти, имя даешь ей: покой.
Нам, из ничтожества вызванным творчества словом тревожным,
Жизнь для волненья дана: жизнь и волненье – одно.
Тот, кого миновали общие смуты, заботу
Сам вымышляет себе: лиру, палитру, резец;
Мира невежда, младенец, как будто закон его чуя,
Первым стенаньем качать нудит свою колыбель!

* * *

Филида с каждою зимою,
Зимою новою своей,
Пугает большей наготою
Своих старушечьих плечей.

И, Афродита гробовая,
Подходит, словно к ложу сна,
За ризой ризу опуская,
К одру последнему она.

TO A SAGE

Between cold death and the storms of life, in vain
you search for a port, philosopher, to call it peace.
Raised from the void by creation's unquiet voice,
life is given for passion: passion and life are one.
He who escapes the common turmoil still decrees
cares enough for himself, with lyre or chisel or brush;
ignorant of the world, the baby senses its laws
and calls for its cot to be rocked with its newborn cries.

* * *

Phyllis with each returning winter
makes a new winter of her own,
baring yet more her ancient shoulders
to freeze the thoughts of all the town.

So this funereal Aphrodite,
laying aside veil after veil,
as if preparing for a night's rest,
comes to her final resting place.

БОКАЛ

Полный влагой искрометной,
Зашипел ты, мой бокал!
И покрыл туман приветный
Твой озябнувший кристалл…
Ты не встречен братьей шумной,
Буйных оргий властелин, –
Сластолюбец вольнодумный,
Я сегодня пью один.

Чем душа моя богата,
Всё твое, о друг Аи!
Ныне мысль моя не сжата
И свободны сны мои;
За струею вдохновенной
Не рассеян данник твой
Бестолково оживленной,
Разногласною толпой.

Мой восторг неосторожный
Не обидит никого;
Не откроет дружбе ложной
Таин счастья моего;
Не смутит глупцов ревнивых
И торжественных невежд
Излияньем горделивых
Иль святых моих надежд!

Вот теперь со мной беседуй,
Своенравная струя!
Упоенья проповедуй
Иль отравы бытия;
Сердцу милые преданья
Благодатно оживи
Или прошлые страданья
Мне на память призови!

GOBLET

Sparkling with iridescent vapour,
goblet, how you bubble and foam!
Numb with cold your crystal glimmers
through a mist that warms the soul.
Here no noisy confraternity
hails you as the orgy's chief –
free in mind, a pleasure seeker,
tonight I drink by myself.

All the treasures of my spirit
come from you, Cliquot my friend!
Now my thoughts are not imprisoned
by people, and my dreams fly free;
drinking you, inspired creation,
your vassal is not led astray
by the senseless animation,
the Babel of society.

If I cannot hide my rapture,
who is there to take offence?
No false friendships can uncover
the secrets of my happiness.
I shall not shock pompous fatheads
or kindle idiots' jealousy
by pouring out my noble-hearted
sacred hopes for all to see.

So now, come, be my companion,
speak to me, unrivalled wine,
teach me the exhilaration
or the bitterness of being;
compassionately give new life to
memories that I hold most dear,
or call to mind the long forgotten
sufferings of other years.

О бокал уединенья!
Не усилены тобой
Пошлой жизни впечатленья,
Словно чашей круговой;
Плодородней, благородней,
Дивной силой будишь ты
Откровенья преисподней
Иль небесные мечты.

И один я пью отныне!
Не в людском шуму пророк –
В немотствующей пустыне
Обретает свет высок!
Не в бесплодном развлеченьи
Общежительных страстей –
В одиноком упоеньи
Мгла падет с его очей!

Goblet of solitude! You never
give new credence to the cheap
impressions of everyday existence
like some common loving cup;
nobler, richer, you awaken
with a wonder-working might
heavenly dreams or revelations
of regions hidden from our sight.

Let me drink alone henceforward!
Shunning crowds, the prophet sees
the bright light of inspiration
in the silent wilderness.
Not the old sterile distractions,
common passions, social lies,
but solitary intoxication
clears the mist that clouds our eyes!

* * *

Были бури, непогоды,
Да младые были годы!

В день ненастный, час гнетучий
Грудь подымет вздох могучий;

Вольной песнью разольется,
Скорбь-невзгода распоется!

А как век то, век то старый
Обручится с лютой карой,

Груз двойной с груди усталой
Уж не сбросит вздох удалый:

Не положишь ты на голос
С черной мыслью белый волос!

* * *

I have known them, storms, bad weather,
but I was young then, was another!

When day is dark and time oppresses,
Up from the breast a strong sigh rises

and spills out in a song of freedom,
scattering grief and care in singing!

But when the century brings old age
coupled with an avenging fate,

no vigorous sigh can then unseat
these twin weights from the weary breast:

in vain you seek to harmonise
white hair and a sombre mind!

* * *

На что вы, дни! Юдольный мир явленья
    Свои не изменит!
Все ведомы, и только повторенья
    Грядущее сулит.

Недаром ты металась и кипела,
    Развитием спеша,
Свой подвиг ты свершила прежде тела,
    Безумная душа!

И, тесный круг подлунных впечатлений
    Сомкнувшая давно,
Под веяньем возвратных сновидений
    Ты дремлешь; а оно

Бессмысленно глядит, как утро встанет,
    Без нужды ночь сменя,
Как в мрак ночной бесплодный вечер канет,
    Венец пустого дня!

* * *

Days! What's the use! This earthly life will never
     bring anything unknown!
All is familiar, and we can only
     expect the same again.

Poor foolish soul! Why be in such a hurry?
     Too hot for your own good,
you grew to your noble maturity
     before the body could!

And having soon run through the narrow gamut
     of worldly incident,
cradled by dreams of life as once you knew it,
     you fall asleep, but it,

the body, wildly staring, sees the morning
     follow the night in vain,
then darkness swallow up the sterile evening,
     crowning the vacant day.

КОТТЕРИИ

Братайтеся, к взаимной обороне
Ничтожностей своих вы рождены;
Но дар прямой не брат у вас в притоне,
Бездарные писцы-хлопотуны!
Наоборот, союзным на благое,
Реченного достойные друзья,
«Аминь, аминь, – вещал он вам, – где трое
Вы будете – не буду с вами я.»

АХИЛЛ

Влага Стикса закалила
Дикой силы полноту
И кипящего Ахилла
Бою древнему явила
Уязвимым лишь в пяту.

Обречен борьбе верховной,
Ты ли, долею своей
Равен с ним, боец духовный,
Сын купели новых дней?

Омовен ее водою,
Знай, страданью над собою
Волю полную ты дал,
И одной пятой своею
Невредим ты, если ею
На живую веру стал!

CLIQUES

You live to guarantee for one another
your non-existent gifts, so fraternise;
but don't expect real writers in your cavern,
poor band of scribblers, busy with your lies!
Oh no, my worthy friends of what was spoken,
huddling together, hear the Master who
now says: "Where two or three of you are gathered,
verily, I shall not be with you."

ACHILLES

Hardened in the Styx's waters,
Achilles was a man of steel
prepared to face those ancient battles
with all his savage strength; the archers
could only wound him through the heel.

Doomed to put up a greater struggle,
baptised to live in modern days,
are you his equal in your powers,
you who uphold the spirit's cause?

With the blessing of this baptism,
know you have given suffering
mastery of your life and fate.
And you are invulnerable only
in your heel, once you have set it
into the way of living faith!

* * *

Сначала мысль, воплощена
В поэму сжатую поэта,
Как дева юная, темна
Для невнимательного света;
Потом, осмелившись, она
Уже увертлива, речиста,
Со всех сторон своих видна,
Как искушенная жена
В свободной прозе романиста;
Болтунья старая, затем
Она, подъемля крик нахальный,
Плодит в полемике журнальной
Давно уж ведомое всем.

* * *

Еще, как патриарх, не древен я; моей
Главы не умастил таинственный елей:
Непосвященных рук бездарно возложенье!
И я даю тебе мое благословенье
Во знаменьи ином, о дева красоты!
Под этой розою главой склонись, о ты,
Подобие цветов царицы ароматной,
В залог румяных дней и доли благодатной.

* * *

Thought, when embodied first of all
in the dense lines of poetry
is enigmatic, a young girl
in the unthinking public eye;
then, growing bolder, she steps out
already skilled and eloquent,
a woman who has come of age,
clear to the view on every side –
the novelist's untrammelled page;
lastly, a gossipy old dame,
she fills the press's echoing dome
with strident disputatious cries –
we've heard it all a thousand times.

* * *

I am not yet ancient as a patriarch; my head
has not been touched with sacrificial oils:
worthless the laying on of hands unconsecrated!
And I bestow on you my benediction
under a different sign, maiden of loveliness!
Incline your head beneath this rose, oh you,
likeness of the sweet-smelling queen of flowers,
in earnest of shining days and life's abundance.

* * *

Толпе тревожный день приветен, но страшна
Ей ночь безмолвная. Боится в ней она
Раскованной мечты видений своевольных.
Не легкокрылых грез, детей волшебной тьмы,
　　Видений дня боимся мы,
　　Людских сует, забот юдольных.

　　Ощупай возмущенный мрак –
　　Исчезнет, с пустотой сольется
　　Тебя пугающий призрак,
И заблужденью чувств твой ужас улыбнется.

О сын фантазии! ты благодатных фей
Счастливый баловень, и там, в заочном мире,
Веселый семьянин, привычный гость на пире
　　Неосязаемых властей!
　　Мужайся, не слабей душою
　　Перед заботою земною:
Ей исполинский вид дает твоя мечта;
Коснися облака нетрепетной рукою –
Исчезнет; а за ним опять перед тобою
Обители духов откроются врата.

* * *

Fretful daytime pleases the multitude,
but they dread the silent night. They fear
capricious visions in their dreams unloosed.
It is not airy dreams we fear, sweet fruit
      of darkness, but visions of the day,
      frets and cares of the narrow vale.

      Just test the turbid obscurity –
      the apparitions that you feared
      vanish into vacuity,
and your terror smiles at your deluded mind.

Oh son of fantasy, you are the happiest
child of the kindly fairies, and in that house
      a happy, well-loved guest
      at the table of unknown powers.
      Take courage, do not let your soul
      shrink in the face of earthly worries:
your dreaming figures them in monstrous shapes;
but touch the cloud with fearless hands, and lo!
they disappear, and once again the gates
of the house of spirits open wide for you.

* * *

Здравствуй, отрок сладкогласный!
Твой рассвет зарей прекрасной
Озаряет Аполлон!
Честь возникшему пииту!
Малолетную хариту
Ранней лирой тронул он.

С утра дней счастлив и славен,
Кто тебе, мой мальчик, равен?
Только жавронок живой,
Чуткой грудию своею,
С первым солнцем, полный всею
Наступающей весной!

* * *

Greetings! sweet-tongued boy, your rising,
illuminated by Apollo,
is radiant with the morning light!
All honour to the youthful poet!
With his awakening lyre he touches
a young and graceful maiden's heart.

Happy and feted at life's dawning,
who can compete with you, young singer?
Only the bird of life, the lark,
delicately strong at sunrise,
full of the coming spring, proclaiming
day that puts to flight the dark.

* * *

Что за звуки? Мимоходом
Ты поешь перед народом,
Старец нищий и слепой!
И, как псов враждебных стая,
Чернь тебя обстала злая,
Издеваясь над тобой.

А с тобой издавна тесен
Был союз камены песен,
И беседовал ты с ней,
Безымянной, роковою,
С дня, как в первый раз тобою
Был услышан соловей.

Бедный старец! слышу чувство
В сильной песне... Но искусство...
Старцев старее оно;
Эти радости, печали –
Музыкальные скрыжали
Выражают их давно!

Опрокинь же свой треножник!
Ты избранник, не художник!
Попеченья гений твой
Да отложит в здешнем мире:
Там, быть может, в горнем клире,
Звучен будет голос твой!

* * *

What sounds are these? Too cheaply
you sing before the people,
poor blind old man.
Like a pack of mean dogs growling,
the hostile mob surrounds you,
mocking your strain.

Yet you have been an intimate
friend of the muse of singing –
she wished you well,
that nameless, fateful goddess
from the day your ears were opened
to the nightingale.

Poor old man! I can hear the feeling
in your strong song… But art's teaching
is older than old men;
they were there, these joys, this heartache,
in the chronicles of music
in days long gone.

So cast to earth your tripod!
A prophet, no mere artist,
let your genius adjourn
its task in our dismal present:
but up there in the empyrean
may your voice one day resound!

***

Всё мысль да мысль! Художник бедный слова!
О жрец ее! тебе забвенья нет;
Всё тут, да тут и человек, и свет,
И смерть, и жизнь, и правда без покрова.
Резец, орган, кисть! счастлив, кто влеком
К ним чувственным, за грань их не ступая!
Есть хмель ему на празднике мирском!
Но пред тобой, как пред нагим мечом,
Мысль, острый луч! бледнеет жизнь земная.

* * *

Thought, yet more thought! Poor artist of the word,
thought's priest! For you there can be no forgetting:
it's all here – here are people and the world
and death and life and truth without a veil.
Ah! chisel, cello, brush, happy the man
drawn to you by his senses, going no further!
He can drink freely at the world's great feast!
But in your presence, thought, in your sharp rays,
before your unsheathed sword, our life grows pale.

СКУЛЬПТОР

Глубокий взор вперив на камень,
Художник нимфу в нем прозрел,
И пробежал по жилам пламень,
И к ней он сердцем полетел.

Но, бесконечно вожделенный,
Уже он властвует собой:
Неторопливый, постепенный
Резец с богини сокровенной
Кору снимает за корой.

В заботе сладостно-туманной
Не час, не день, не год уйдет,
А с предугаданной, с желанной
Покров последний не падет,

Покуда, страсть уразумея
Под лаской вкрадчивой резца,
Ответным взором Галатея
Не увлечет, желаньем рдея,
К победе неги мудреца.

SCULPTOR

Plunging his gaze into the stone,
the artist sees the nymph within,
an ardent flame runs through his veins,
and his heart longs to touch her then.

His desire for her is infinite,
but the sculptor holds himself in check,
unhurrying, deliberate, quiet,
he strips off all the veils that hide
the goddess deep within the rock.

Hours and days and years go past
in his delicious, dim travail,
but from the guessed-at, wished-for shape
he cannot tear the final veil

until one day Galatea sees
the passion beneath the cool caress,
and blushing with an answering gaze,
full of desire, she leads the sage
to the triumph of voluptuousness.

ОСЕНЬ

1

И вот сентябрь! замедля свой восход,
    Сияньем хладным солнце блещет,
И луч его в зерцале зыбком вод
    Неверным золотом трепещет.
Седая мгла виется вкруг холмов;
    Росой затоплены равнины;
Желтеет сень кудрявая дубов,
    И красен круглый лист осины;
Умолкли птиц живые голоса,
Безмолвен лес, беззвучны небеса!

2

И вот сентябрь! и вечер года к нам
    Подходит. На поля и горы
Уже мороз бросает по утрам
    Свои сребристые узоры.
Пробудится ненастливый Эол;
    Пред ним помчится прах летучий,
Качаяся, завоет роща, дол
    Покроет лист ее падучий,
И набегут на небо облака,
И, потемнев, запенится река.

3

Прощай, прощай, сияние небес!
    Прощай, прощай, краса природы!
Волшебного шептанья полный лес,
    Златочешуйчатые воды!

AUTUMN

1

September's here! The sun each morning wakes
    a little later, its rays are colder,
and in the shaky mirror of the lake
    it glitters tremulous and golden.
Grey vapour shrouds the hilltops, and the dew
    drenches the flat lands by the river;
The fretted oak-trees cast a yellowing shade,
    and the red leaves of aspen shiver;
The birds no longer overflow with life,
the forests and the skies have lost their voice.

2

September's here! The evening of the year
    is now upon us. Frost at morning
already spreads its silver filigree
    over the fields and hills, and stormy
Aeolus will awaken from his sleep,
    driving the flying dust before him,
the wood will toss and roar, its falling leaves
    will strew the swampy valley bottom,
and clouds will rise to fill the heavenly dome,
and waters will grow dark in froth and foam.

3

Farewell, farewell, you brilliant summer skies!
    Farewell, farewell to nature's splendour!
The waters gleaming in their golden scales,
    the woods with their enchanted murmur!

Веселый сон минутных летних нег!
    Вот эхо в рощах обнаженных
Секирою тревожит дровосек,
    И скоро, снегом убеленных,
Своих дубров и холмов зимний вид
Застылый ток туманно отразит.

4

А между тем досужий селянин
    Плод годовых трудов сбирает;
Сметав в стога скошенный злак долин,
    С серпом он в поле поспешает.
Гуляет серп. На сжатых бороздах
    Снопы стоят в копнах блестящих
Иль тянутся вдоль жнивы, на возах,
    Под тяжкой ношею скрыпящих,
И хлебных скирд золотоверхий град
Подъемлется кругом крестьянских хат.

5

Дни сельского, святого торжества!
    Овины весело дымятся,
И цеп стучит, и с шумом жернова
    Ожившей мельницы крутятся.
Иди, зима! на строги дни себе
    Припас оратай много блага:
Отрадное тепло в его избе,
    Хлеб-соль и пенистая брага;
С семьей своей вкусит он без забот
Своих трудов благословенный плод!

Oh happy dream of fleeting summer joys!
          The woodmen's axes are disturbing
the echoes in the emaciated groves,
          and all too soon the frozen river
will be a mirror for the misty oaks
and the hills in their white covering of snow.

          4

And now the villagers will find the time
          to gather in their hard-earned harvest;
Hay in the valley is stacked up into piles,
          and in the corn the sickle dances.
Over the furrows, once the grain is cleared,
          sheaves in stooks stand high and gleaming,
or else they trundle past the empty field
          on loaded carts wearily creaking.
The golden summits of the shining ricks
rise up around the peasants' huddled shacks.

          5

The village people celebrate the day!
          The barns steam merrily, the clatter
of flails awakes the mill-stones from their sleep,
          and noisily they turn and chatter.
Let the cold come! the farmer has saved up
          supplies to last him through the winter:
his hut is warm, the bread, the salt, the cup
          of beer make welcome all who enter;
without a care his family now can eat
the blessed fruit of work through summer's heat.

6

А ты, когда вступаешь в осень дней,
    Оратай жизненного поля,
И пред тобой во благостыне всей
    Является земная доля;
Когда тебе житейские бразды,
    Труд бытия вознаграждая,
Готовятся подать свои плоды
    И спеет жатва дорогая,
И в зернах дум ее сбираешь ты,
Судеб людских достигнув полноты, —

7

Ты так же ли, как земледел, богат?
    И ты, как он, с надеждой сеял;
И ты, как он, о дальнем дне наград
    Сны позлащенные лелеял…
Любуйся же, гордись восставшим им!
    Считай свои приобретенья!…
Увы! к мечтам, страстям, трудам мирским
    Тобой скопленные презренья,
Язвительный, неотразимый стыд
Души твоей обманов и обид!

8

Твой день взошел, и для тебя ясна
    Вся дерзость юных легковерий;
Испытана тобою глубина
    Людских безумств и лицемерий.

6

And you, a labourer in the field of life,
    when you too move into your autumn
and see the blessings of your earthly time
    spread out abundantly before you;
when the rich acres ploughed by work and cares
    display the profits of your labours,
rewarding you for all the weary years
    and you can reap the precious harvest,
gathering the grain of long-considered thought,
tasting the fullness of our human lot, –

7

Are you rich like the countryman who sowed
    so full of hope? Like him you scattered
the seed and cherished golden dreams that showed
    you rich rewards far in the future...
Now you behold that day; greet it with pride
    and count your painful acquisitions!
Alas, your passions, your dreams, your arduous road
    are buried in scorn, and your condition
is the soul's irresistible disgrace,
the sting of disappointment on your face!

8

Your day has risen; now you can clearly see
    the arrogance, the gullibility
of youth, and you have plumbed the yawning sea
    of people's madness and hypocrisy.

Ты, некогда всех увлечений друг,
Сочувствий пламенный искатель,
Блистательных туманов царь – и вдруг
Бесплодных дебрей созерцатель,
Один с тоской, которой смертный стон
Едва твоей гордыней задушен.

9

Но если бы негодованья крик,
Но если б вопль тоски великой
Из глубины сердечныя возник
Вполне торжественный и дикой, –
Костями бы среди своих забав
Содроглась ветреная младость,
Играющий младенец, зарыдав,
Игрушку б выронил, и радость
Покинула б чело его навек,
И заживо б в нем умер человек!

10

Зови ж теперь на праздник честный мир!
Спеши, хозяин тороватый!
Проси, сажай гостей своих за пир
Затейливый, замысловатый!
Что лакомству пророчит он утех!
Каким разнообразьем брашен
Блистает он!.. Но вкус один во всех,
И, как могила, людям страшен;
Садись один и тризну соверши
По радостям земным твоей души!

You, once enthusiasm's faithful friend,
    ardently seeking fellow-feeling,
a king of brilliant vapours – in the end
    you contemplate a sterile thicket
alone with misery, whose mortal groan
is barely muffled by your haughty soul.

9

But if your indignation's potent cry,
    or if a howl of urgent longing
should rise out of the heart's dark misery,
    solemn and wild amid the thronging
young boys and girls at their capricious games,
    their bones would shake in fear, the baby
would drop its toys and in the midst of play
    set up a roar of pain, all gladness
would vanish from its face, humanity
would die in it before death set it free.

10

Be open-handed then, invite them all
    to join the feast, those splendid people!
Let them all take their places in the hall
    around the gold-encrusted table!
What tasty titbits you can offer them!
    What a display of dishes gleaming
so variously! But they all taste the same
    and like the grave they make us tremble;
sit there alone, perform the funeral rites
for your soul's worldly, transient delights.

11

Какое же потом в груди твоей
    Ни водворится озаренье,
Чем дум и чувств ни разрешится в ней
    Последнее вихревращенье –
Пусть в торжестве насмешливом своем
    Ум бесполезный сердца трепет
Угомонит и тщетных жалоб в нем
    Удушит запоздалый лепет,
И примешь ты, как лучший жизни клад,
Дар опыта, мертвящий душу хлад.

12

Иль, отряхнув видения земли
    Порывом скорби животворной,
Ее предел завидя невдали,
    Цветущий брег за мглою черной,
Возмездий край, благовестящим снам
    Доверясь чувством обновленным,
И бытия мятежным голосам,
    В великом гимне примиренным,
Внимающий, как арфам, коих строй
Превыспренний не понят был тобой, –

13

Пред Промыслом оправданным ты ниц
    Падешь с признательным смиреньем,
С надеждою, не видящей границ,
    И утоленным разуменьем, –

11

Whatever illumination in years to come
        may take possession of your fancy,
whatever the last vortex of your thoughts
        and feelings may one day give birth to –
let your triumphant and sarcastic mind
        suppress your heart's vain tremors
and bridle the unprofitable wind
        of late laments. Then see the treasure
you will receive, the greatest gift of life,
experience, which binds the soul in ice.

12

Or else, in a life-giving surge of grief,
        casting aside all earthly visions,
seeing their boundaries, and not far off,
        a golden land beyond the darkness,
a place of redress, with a heart renewed
        dreaming dreams of benediction,
and hearing those tumultous voices tuned
        to hymns of reconciliation,
like harps whose over-lofty harmony
is unintelligible to your human ear, –

13

before a vindicated Providence
        you will bow down, humble and thankful,
with an unbounded hope and with the sense
        that you have reached some understanding –

Знай, внутренней своей вовеки ты
 Не передашь земному звуку
И легких чад житейской суеты
 Не посвятишь в свою науку;
Знай, горняя иль дольная, она
Нам на земле не для земли дана.

14

Вот буйственно несется ураган,
 И лес подъемлет говор шумный,
И пенится, и ходит океан,
 И в берег бьет волной безумной;
Так иногда толпы ленивый ум
 Из усыпления выводит
Глас, пошлый глас, вещатель общих дум,
 И звучный отзыв в ней находит,
Но не найдет отзыва тот глагол,
Что страстное земное перешел.

15

Пускай, приняв неправильный полет
 И вспять стези не обретая,
Звезда небес в бездонность утечет;
 Пусть заменит ее другая;
Не явствует земле ущерб одной,
 Не поражает ухо мира
Падения ее далекий вой,
 Равно как в высотах эфира
Ее сестры новорожденный свет
И небесам восторженный привет!

but know: you never will communicate
        your vision to your fellow-mortals;
their frivolous souls will never appreciate
        true knowledge in society's bustle;
knowledge of mountain peaks or of the deeps
is not for earth, earth has no place for it.

14

The hurricane goes hurtling through the void,
        the forest raises up its voice in anger,
the ocean foams and rages and its mad
        breakers explode against the shingle;
so sometimes the dull rabble's idle minds
        are woken from their torpid slumber
by the crude voice of commonplace, that finds
        a sonorous echo in their blether,
but there will be no echo for the word
that goes beyond the passions of the world.

15

What if a star from heaven disappears
        into the chasm of nothing, missing
its way, and never finds its place again;
        another one replaces it unheeded.
One star the less is nothing to the earth,
        our people are too hard of hearing
to catch the distant howling of its death
        or see the brightness of a star appearing
new born amid the sisters of the sky
and greeting them with rapturous melody!

16

Зима идет, и тощая земля
В широких лысинах бессилья,
И радостно блиставшие поля
Златыми класами обилья,
Со смертью жизнь, богатство с нищетой
Все образы годины бывшей
Сравняются под снежной пеленой,
Однообразно их покрывшей, –
Перед тобой таков отныне свет,
Но в нем тебе грядущей жатвы нет!

* * *

Благословен святое возвестивший!
Но в глубине разврата не погиб
Какой-нибудь неправедный изгиб
Сердец людских пред нами обнаживший.
Две области сияния и тьмы
Исследовать равно стремимся мы.
Плод яблони со древа упадает:
Закон небес постигнул человек!
Так в дикий смысл порока посвящает
Нас иногда один его намек.

16

Winter draws on, and over the sick earth
    impotence stretches with a shiver,
and furrows overflow with golden ears,
    and all the cornfields gaily glitter.
Life and death, want and wealth lie side by side –
    all the variety of the year now vanished
is equalised beneath a snowy shroud
    that hides it in indifferent sameness –
thus all things will appear to you henceforth,
but you will reap no harvest from the earth.

'The lost star' of stanza 15 is a reference to Pushkin's death in a duel,
which happened while Baratynsky was writing this poem. Pushkin
also wrote a famous poem entitled 'Autumn'.

       * * *

Blessed be he who speaks of what is sacred!
But in the depths of vice some perverse twist
of human hearts remains that still can make us
aware of what lies hidden in our midst.
We strive with equal zeal to understand
the sun-illuminated and the midnight land.
An apple falling from the tree of knowledge
revealed to the first man the laws of heaven.
Just so the merest intimation sometimes
unveils the wild significance of evil.

РИФМА

Когда на играх Олимпийских,
На стогнах греческих недавних городов,
Он пел, питомец муз, он пел среди валов
Народа, жадного восторгов мусикийских;
    В нем вера полная в сочувствие жила.
    Свободным и широким метром,
    Как жатва, зыблемая ветром,
    Его гармония текла.
Толпа вниманием окована была,
    Пока, могучим сотрясеньем
Вдруг побежденная, плескала без конца
    И струны звучные певца
    Дарила новым вдохновеньем.

    Когда на греческий амвон,
    Когда на римскую трибуну
Оратор восходил, и славословил он
Или оплакивал народную фортуну,
И устремлялися все взоры на него,
    И силой слова своего
Вития властвовал народным произволом;
    Он знал, кто он; он ведать мог,
    Какой могучий правит бог
    Его торжественным глаголом.
    Но нашей мысли торжищ нет,
    Но нашей мысли нет форума!...
    Меж нас не ведает поэт,
    Высок полет его иль нет,
    Велика ль творческая дума?

    Сам судия и подсудимый,
    Скажи: твой беспокойный жар –
    Смешной недуг иль высший дар?
    Реши вопрос неразрешимый!

RHYME

When once the poet at the Olympic
contests gave voice above the squares
of those long-gone Greek cities, sang amidst
the waves of people all athirst for music,
he felt hearts beat in sympathy with him
and in a metre free and wide
like cornfields blowing in the wind,
his melody flowed on. The public
was held transfixed then by their rapt attention
till suddenly, swept by emotion,
the crowd burst out in infinite applause,
enriching with new inspiration
the bard's melodious strings and voice.

When in the agora or the senate
the orator stood to champion or lament
the public weal, all eyes that very minute
were fixed on him, the power of his speech
subdued the people's fickle moods.
He knew his part, he knew what mighty will
dictated his all-conquering words.
But *our* thoughts know no Olympic car,
no forum and no agora!
Our poets cannot tell how far
their flight will reach, and cannot know
whether their work ranks high or low.

Both judge and prisoner at the bar,
tell me, is your unquiet flame
a lofty gift or foolish game?
Answer this riddle if you can!

Среди безжизненного сна,
Средь гробового хлада света,
Своею ласкою поэта
Ты, Рифма! радуешь одна.
Подобно голубю ковчега,
Одна ему, с родного брега,
Живую ветвь приносишь ты;
Одна с божественным порывом
Миришь его твоим отзывом
И признаешь его мечты!

In the dark sleep of lifelessness,
amid the world's sepulchral cold,
the poet finds some joy, sweet rhyme,
in your caress, in you alone!
You, like the faithful dove, bring back
a green branch to the waiting ark
and place it in his eager hand;
you only with your echoing voice
give inspiration a human face
and bring his dream to land.

OTHER POEMS

ПРИЗНАНИЕ

Притворной нежности не требуй от меня:
Я сердца моего не скрою хлад печальный.
Ты права, в нем уж нет прекрасного огня
    Моей любви первоначальной.
Напрасно я себе на память приводил
И милый образ твой и прежние мечтанья:
    Безжизненны мои воспоминанья,
    Я клятвы дал, но дал их выше сил.

    Я не пленен красавицей другою,
Мечты ревнивые от сердца удали;
Но годы долгие в разлуке протекли,
Но в бурях жизненных развлекся я душою.
    Уж ты жила неверной тенью в ней;
Уже к тебе взывал я редко, принужденно,
    И пламень мой, слабея постепенно,
    Собою сам погас в душе моей.
Верь, жалок я один. Душа любви желает,
    Но я любить не буду вновь;
Вновь не забудусь я: вполне упоевает
    Нас только первая любовь.

Грущу я; но и грусть минует, знаменуя
Судьбины полную победу надо мной;
Кто знает? мнением сольюся я с толпой;
Подругу, без любви – кто знает? – изберу я.
На брак обдуманный я руку ей подам
    И в храме стану рядом с нею,
Невинной, преданной, быть может, лучшим снам,
    И назову ее моею;
И весть к тебе придет, но не завидуй нам:
Обмена тайных дум не будет между нами,
Душевным прихотям мы воли не дадим:
    Мы не сердца под брачными венцами,
    Мы жребии свои соединим.

AN ADMISSION

Do not demand false tenderness from me:
        I won't conceal my heart's sad coldness,
that it no longer burns with the fine flame
        of love I felt in the beginning.
In vain I summoned to my memory
        my old dreams and your sweet appearance:
        my memories are devoid of life,
        I swore an oath, but cannot keep it.

I am not the servant of another beauty.
Drive from your heart the dreams of jealousy;
but I have been long years apart from you,
and in life's storms my soul has grown distracted.
With time you came to seem a fleeting shadow;
I sighed for you less often, less sincerely,
        and my flame, gradually dwindling,
        has gone out of its own accord.
Believe me, I am sad alone. The soul
wants love. But I shall never love again;
never forget myself: only first love
        can bring us that sweet ecstasy.

I grieve; but grief will pass, and this will be
destiny's final triumph over me;
Who knows? I'll come to share the crowd's opinion;
and without love – who knows? – I'll choose a partner,
give her my hand to seal a match of reason
        and stand beside her in the temple
while she, perhaps, all innocent, dreams sweetly,
        and I shall call her mine;
and you will hear of it; but do not envy us:
we shall not share secret thoughts nor let
        our dearest wishes have their way,
our hearts will not be wedded at the altar,
only our destinies will be united.

Прощай! Мы долго шли дорогою одною;
Путь новый я избрал, путь новый избери;
Печаль бесплодную рассудком усмири
И не вступай, молю, в напрасный суд со мною.
    Не властны мы в самих себе
    И, в молодые наши леты,
    Даем поспешные обеты,
Смешные, может быть, всевидящей судьбе.

Farewell! For years we followed the same road;
now I have taken a new one, be like me.
Let reason dull the edge of pointless sorrow,
and please don't waste your time in argument.
      We cannot choose what we shall be
      and in our youthful days
      make hasty vows, that seem, who knows,
mere folly to the all-seeing eye of fate.

БУРЯ

Завыла буря; хлябь морская
Клокочет и ревет, и черные валы
   Идут, до неба восставая,
Бьют, гневно пеняся, в прибрежные скалы.

   Чья неприязненная сила,
   Чья своевольная рука
   Сгустила в тучи облака
И на краю небес ненастье зародила?
   Кто, возмутив природы чин,
Горами влажными на землю гонит море?
Не тот ли злобный дух, геенны властелин,
   Что по вселенной розлил горе,
   Что человека подчинил
Желаньям, немощи, страстям и разрушенью
   И на творенье ополчил
   Все силы, данные творенью?
   Земля трепещет перед ним:
Он небо заслонил огромными крылами
   И двигает ревущими водами,
   Бунтующим могуществом своим.

   Когда придет желанное мгновенье?
Когда волнам твоим я вверюсь, океан?
   Но знай: красой далеких стран
Не очаровано мое воображенье.
   Под небом лучшим обрести
   Я лучшей доли не сумею;
   Вновь не смогу душой моею
   В краю цветущем расцвести.
   Меж тем от прихоти судьбины,
Меж тем от медленной отравы бытия,
   В покое раболепном я
   Ждать не хочу своей кончины;

TEMPEST

The storm is howling, and the yawning sea
clatters and roars, and the black breakers race
      to storm the sky,
belabouring with fierce foam the cliff-clad land.

      Whose is the hostile power,
      whose the capricious hand
      that massed the thundering clouds
and raised foul weather in the courts of heaven?
      Who, overturning nature's balance,
      drives watery mountains on the shore?
Is it that evil spirit, lord of torment,
who poured out sorrow on the universe,
      subordinating human souls
to want and weakness, passion and destruction,
and set against creation all the powers
      that had been given to creation?
      Before him the earth shakes.
He veils the sky with his gigantic wings
      and rules the roaring, rushing waves
      with his unruly majesty.

      When will it come, the longed-for moment?
When shall I sail out on your waters, ocean?
No, it is not the beauty of far places
that has enchanted my imagination.
      I do not hope to find a kinder fate
      under some kinder sky.
      My soul will not flower again
      in some flower-enchanted land.
      But let me not await my end
      from fate's caprice or life's slow pain
      in slavish quietness.

На яростных волнах, в борьбе со гневом их
Она отраднее гордыне человека!
   Как жаждал радостей младых
   Я на заре младого века,
Так ныне, океан, я жажду бурь твоих!

Волнуйся, восставай на каменные грани;
Он веселит меня, твой грозный, дикий рев,
   Как зов к давно желанной брани,
Как мощного врага мне чем-то лестный гнев.

Death is more pleasing to our human pride
among the frenzied waves, facing their rage!
        As in the dawn of youth
        I thirsted for youth's joys,
now, ocean, I am thirsty for your tempests.

Swirl and rise up against the rocky shores;
your fearful untamed roar gladdens my ears,
a summons to a long-awaited war,
or a great enemy's strangely flattering anger.

ПОСЛЕДНЯЯ СМЕРТЬ

Есть бытие; но именем каким
Его назвать? Ни сон оно, ни бденье;
Меж них оно, и в человеке им
С безумием граничит разуменье.
Он в полноте понятья своего,
А между тем, как волны, на него,
Одни других мятежней, своенравней,
Видения бегут со всех сторон,
Как будто бы своей отчизны давней
Стихийному смятенью отдан он;
Но иногда, мечтой воспламененный,
Он видит свет, другим не откровенный.

Созданье ли болезненной мечты,
Иль дерзкого ума соображенье,
Во глубине полночной темноты
Представшее очам моим виденье?
Не ведаю; но предо мной тогда
Раскрылися грядущие года;
События вставали, развивались,
Волнуяся подобно облакам,
И полными эпохами являлись
От времени до времени очам,
И наконец я видел без покрова
Последнюю судьбу всего живого.

Сначала мир явил мне дивный сад;
Везде искусств, обилия приметы;
Близ веси весь и подле града град,
Везде дворцы, театры, водометы,
Везде народ, и хитрый свой закон
Стихии все признать заставил он.

ULTIMATE DEATH

There is a way of being; but how can I
describe it? It is neither sleep, nor waking;
somewhere between the two, we walk the line
that separates insanity from reason.
Our mind is fully in control,
but at the same time we see visions roll –
each wilder, more capricious than the last –
from every side upon our heads, as if
we were abandoned to the elements
that rage across our long-lost native land;
but sometimes, with an eye quickened by dreams,
we see a light that others cannot see.

Was it the fiction of a feverish dream
or the creation of my reckless mind,
this vision that rose up before my eyes
in the black depths of night? I cannot say,
but at that time I seemed to see revealed
what was to come in future years, events
ascended into air, developing
and shifting like the clouds, and whole epochs
from time to time lay open to my sight,
and finally I saw without a veil
the ultimate fate of everything alive.

At first the world was like a magic garden;
on every side were the marks of art and wealth –
villages, towns and cities, everywhere
palaces, fountains, theatres, everywhere
people, and all the elements obeyed
the ingenious laws that they laid down. Already

Уж он морей мятежные пучины
На островах искусственных селил,
Уж рассекал небесные равнины
По прихоти им вымышленных крил;
Всё на земле движением дышало,
Всё на земле как будто ликовало.

Исчезнули бесплодные года,
Оратаи по воле призывали
Ветра, дожди, жары и холода,
И верною сторицей воздавали
Посевы им, и хищный зверь исчез
Во тьме лесов, и в высоте небес,
И в бездне вод, сраженный человеком,
И царствовал повсюду светлый мир.
Вот, мыслил я, прельщенный дивным веком,
Вот разума великолепный пир!
Врагам его и в стыд и в поученье,
Вот до чего достигло просвещенье!

Прошли века. Яснеть очам моим
Видение другое начинало:
Что человек? что вновь открыто им?
Я гордо мнил, и что же мне предстало?
Наставшую эпоху я с трудом
Постигнуть мог смутившимся умом.
Глаза мои людей не узнавали;
Привыкшие к обилью дольных благ,
На всё они спокойные взирали,
Что суеты рождало в их отцах,
Что мысли их, что страсти их, бывало,
Влечением всесильным увлекало.

they had created artificial islands
floating upon the unruly depths of ocean.
Already they were soaring through the heights
of heaven on wilful wings of their invention.
All things on earth were breathing a new life.
All things on earth seemed lost in exultation.

The barren years were past. The husbandmen
called up at will the winds, the rains, the cold
and heat, and seeds returned a hundredfold
into their hands; the savage beasts had fled
into the forest's night, the ocean's flood,
the sky's immensity, overcome by man,
and the world shone in triumph everywhere.
Here then, I thought, dazed by these golden times,
is the imperishable feast of reason!
Shaming her enemies and teaching them a lesson,
enlightenment has scaled unheard-of heights.

Ages went by, and now a different vision
began to gleam before me. What is mankind?
To what unknown discoveries have we risen?
I proudly thought – but what now filled my mind!
Only with difficulty could my troubled brain
begin to apprehend the coming epoch.
My eyes no longer recognized the people;
accustomed to the golden gifts of fortune,
they gazed on all things imperturbably,
all that of old had stirred their ancestors,
moved thoughts and passions irresistibly.

Желания земные позабыв,
Чуждаяся их грубого влеченья,
Душевных снов, высоких снов призыв
Им заменил другие побужденья,
И в полное владение свое
Фантазия взяла их бытие,
И умственной природе уступила
Телесная природа между них:
Их в эмпирей и в хаос уносила
Живая мысль на крылиях своих;
Но по земле с трудом они ступали,
И браки их бесплодны пребывали.

Прошли века, и тут моим очам
Открылася ужасная картина:
Ходила смерть по суше, по водам,
Свершалася живущего судьбина.
Где люди? где? Скрывалися в гробах!
Как древние столпы на рубежах,
Последние семейства истлевали;
В развалинах стояли города,
По пажитям заглохнувшим блуждали
Без пастырей безумные стада;
С людьми для них исчезло пропитанье;
Мне слышалось их гладное блеянье.

И тишина глубокая вослед
Торжественно повсюду воцарилась,
И в дикую порфиру древних лет
Державная природа облачилась.
Величествен и грустен был позор
Пустынных вод, лесов, долин и гор.
По-прежнему животворя природу,
На небосклон светило дня взошло,

Forgetting all desire for earthly things,
shrinking from such vulgar stimulation,
and deaf to the spirit's call, the voice of dreams,
they acted on a different motivation,
and their whole being was bound hand and foot,
a captive in the hands of fantasy.
An artificial nature had taken the place
of bodily nature for them; they were swept
into the empirium or into chaos on wings
of thought, but on earth they barely crept,
and all their marriages remained unblest.

Ages went by, and now my eyes beheld
a fearful sight: death walked the land and the waves;
the fate of living beings was fulfilled.
Where were the people? Where? Dead in their graves!
Like mouldering columns at the frontiers
the last few families were dying out;
towns stood in ruin, senseless flocks unguarded
wandered the meadows where the weeds ran riot;
their food had vanished with the hands that fed them,
and I could hear their hungry lamentation.

And when their bleating died away, a deep
and solemn silence seized on everything,
and nature, savage and imperial,
put on the purple of antiquity.
Magnificent and gloomy the spectacle
of forests, valleys, mountains, seas unpeopled!
The sun still rose into the firmament
and animated nature as in former days,

Но на земле ничто его восходу
Произнести привета не могло.
Один туман над ней, синея, вился
И жертвою чистительной дымился.

* * *

Мой дар убог, и голос мой не громок,
Но я живу, и на земли мое
Кому-нибудь любезно бытие:
Его найдет далекий мой потомок
В моих стихах; как знать? душа моя
Окажется с душой его в сношенье,
И как нашел я друга в поколенье,
Читателя найду в потомстве я.

but nothing was left on earth to celebrate
its rising. Only mist curled on its face,
blue wreaths of smoke, a cleansing sacrifice.

* * *

My talent is pitiful, my voice not loud,
but I am living; somewhere in the world
someone looks kindly on my life; one day
a distant fellow-man will read my words
and find my being; and, who knows, my soul
will raise an echo in his soul, and I,
who found a friend in my own time,
will find a reader in posterity.

***

К чему невольнику мечтания свободы?
Взгляни: безропотно текут речные воды
В указанных брегах, по склону их русла;
Ель величавая стоит, где возросла,
Невластная сойти. Небесные светила
Назначенным путем неведомая сила
Влечет. Бродячий ветр не волен, и закон
Его летучему дыханью положен.
Уделу своему и мы покорны будем,
Мятежные мечты смирим иль позабудем,
Рабы разумные, послушно согласим
Свои желания со жребием своим –
И будет счастлива, спокойна наша доля.
Безумец! не она ль, не вышняя ли воля
Дарует страсти нам? и не ее ли глас
В их гласе слышим мы? О, тягостна для нас
Жизнь, в сердце бьющая могучею волною
И в грани узкие втесненная судьбою.

***

Болящий дух врачует песнопенье.
Гармонии таинственная власть
Тяжелое искупит заблужденье
И укротит бунтующую страсть.
Душа певца, согласно излитая,
Разрешена от всех своих скорбей;
И чистоту поэзия святая
И мир отдаст причастнице своей.

* * *

What is the freedom of dreams to the prisoner? Look
at the uncomplaining river flowing on
between the appointed banks of its downhill course;
the fir-tree stands majestic where it grew tall
and has no power to move. The lamps of heaven
are drawn in their fixed ways by an unknown power.
The wandering wind is unfree. Its every breath
is subject to law. So let us also submit
to our lot without grumbling. Let us either tame
or forget our rebellious dreams with the wisdom of slaves,
obediently reconciling our desires
with our fate – and we shall live happy and calm.
Madman! Are our passions not given to us
by a higher will? And do we not hear its voice
in their voice? Oh, heavily life weighs us down,
pulsing within our hearts like a raging wave
and confined by fate within its narrow bounds.

* * *

Song heals the aching spirit
and harmony's mysterious power
redeems the heavy load of error
and bridles in the passions' riot.
The singer's soul, poured out in melody,
is freed from every sorrow,
and holy poetry gives purity
and peace to her sad sister.

* * *

Я посетил тебя, пленительная сень,
Не в дни веселые живительного мая,
Когда, зелеными ветвями помавая,
Манишь ты путника в свою густую тень,
    Когда ты веешь ароматом
Тобою бережно взлелеянных цветов, –
    Под очарованный твой кров
    Замедлил я моим возвратом.
В осенней наготе стояли дерева
    И неприветливо чернели;
Хрустела под ногой замерзлая трава,
И листья мертвые, волнуяся, шумели;
    С прохладой резкою дышал
    В лицо мне запах увяданья;
Но не весеннего убранства я искал,
    А прошлых лет воспоминанья.
Душой задумчивый, медлительно я шел
С годов младенческих знакомыми тропами;
Художник опытный их некогда провел.
Увы, рука его изглажена годами!
Стези заглохшие, мечтаешь, пешеход
Случайно протоптал. Сошел я в дол заветный,
Дол, первых дум моих лелеятель приветный!
Пруда знакомого искал красивых вод,
Искал прыгучих вод мне памятной каскады;
    Там, думал я, к душе моей
Толпою полетят виденья прежних дней…
Вотще! лишенные хранительной преграды,
    Далече воды утекли,
    Их ложе поросло травою,
Приют хозяйственный в нем улья обрели,
И легкая тропа исчезла предо мною.
Ни в чем знакомого мой взор не обретал!
Но вот по-прежнему, лесистым косогором,

* * *

Enchanted groves, I came to visit you
not in the joyful time when May enlivens
the meadows and you signal with green branches,
tempting the traveller into your deep shade,
     when you pour out the fragrance
of flowers you have nurtured through the spring –
I let the months slip past before I came
     to seek again your spell-bound shelter.
The trees were standing in their autumn bareness,
     black and unwelcoming, the grass,
stiffened by hoarfrost, crackled underfoot,
and the dead leaves moved in the wind and whispered,
     the biting air breathed in my face
an odour of decay, but I was seeking,
     not the sweet ornaments of springtime,
     but memories of former years.
Slowly I walked, my soul besieged by thoughts,
along the paths familiar from childhood,
long ago traced here by a skilful artist.
Alas! his hand had been effaced by time!
The paths, all overgrown, appeared to me
the trampled signs of casual walks. I found the valley,
the sacred valley, nursemaid to my first thoughts!
I sought the waters of the well-loved pond,
the leaping waters of the great cascade,
so dear to memory, where I hoped to meet
visions of bygone days flocking to greet me.
In vain! now nothing held the water back
     from flowing far beyond its bed,
the place was overgrown with matted grasses
where bees had found a home; faintly the path
went wandering off before my eyes, and nothing
was left to me of all I knew so well!
Then suddenly, as in the days of old,

Дорожка смелая ведет меня… обвал
Вдруг поглотил ее… Я стал
И глубь нежданную измерил грустным взором,
С недоумением искал другой тропы.
Иду я: где беседка тлеет
И в прахе перед ней лежат ее столпы,
Где остов мостика дряхлеет.
И ты, величественный грот,
Тяжело-каменный, постигнут разрушеньем
И угрожаешь уж паденьем,
Бывало, в летний зной прохлады полный свод!
Что ж? пусть минувшее минуло сном летучим!
Еще прекрасен ты, заглохший Элизей,
И обаянием могучим
Исполнен для души моей.
Он не был мыслию, он не был сердцем хладен,
Тот, кто, глубокой неги жаден,
Их своенравный бег тропам сим указал,
Кто, преклоняя слух к таинственному шуму
Сих кленов, сих дубов, в душе своей питал
Ему сочувственную думу.
Давно кругом меня о нем умолкнул слух,
Прияла прах его далекая могила,
Мне память образа его не сохранила,
Но здесь еще живет его доступный дух;
Здесь, друг мечтанья и природы,
Я познаю его вполне:
Он вдохновением волнуется во мне,
Он славить мне велит леса, долины, воды;
Он убедительно пророчит мне страну,
Где я наследую несрочную весну,
Где разрушения следов я не примечу,
Где в сладостной тени невянущих дубров,
У нескудеющих ручьев,
Я тень, священную мне, встречу.

a steep track led me boldly through the woodlands
    down into a ravine; I halted
and sadly scanned this unexpected hollow,
perplexed and searching for another pathway.
    I went on down – a summerhouse
    was rotting, pillars crumbling round it
    and age decaying the bridge's timber.
And you, majestic grotto, in those days
    weighty with stone, have fallen victim
to ruin, and the shady vaults that once
gave shelter from the summer heat, are falling.
Well, let the past be past, a fleeting vision!
You are still fair, weed-grown Elysium,
    and with a mighty fascination
    you speak to my receptive soul.
Not mean of thought nor cold of heart the man
    who, thirsty for a deep contentment,
first drew the plan for these capricious paths,
    and listening to the dreamy music
of oaks and maples, felt his soul expand
    to thoughts in sympathy with theirs.
For years his name has not been spoken near me,
    a distant grave contains his ashes,
no image holds his memory for me,
but here I still can feel his living spirit,
    a lover of nature and of dreams,
    here I can come to know him fully:
he stirs within me like an inspiration,
commanding me to praise the woods, the waters,
the forests, and he tells me of a land
where I shall inherit an unending spring,
where there will be no traces of destruction,
where I shall meet beneath the undying oaks'
    sweet shade, beside unfailing rivers
the man who is for me a sacred shade.

НА ПОСЕВ ЛЕСА

Опять весна; опять смеется луг,
И весел лес своей младой одеждой,
И поселян неутомимый плуг
Браздит поля с покорством и надеждой.

Но нет уже весны в душе моей,
Но нет уже в душе моей надежды,
Уж дольный мир уходит от очей,
Пред вечным днем я опускаю вежды.

Уж та зима главу мою сребрит,
Что греет сев для будущего мира,
Но праг земли не перешел пиит, –
К ее сынам еще взывает лира.

Велик Господь! Он милосерд, но прав:
Нет на земле ничтожного мгновенья;
Прощает он безумию забав,
Но никогда пирам злоумышленья.

Кого измял души моей порыв,
Тот вызвать мог меня на бой кровавый;
Но подо мной, сокрытый ров изрыв,
Свои рога венчал он падшей славой!

Летел душой я к новым племенам,
Любил, ласкал их пустоцветный колос;
Я дни извел, стучась к людским сердцам,
Всех чувств благих я подавал им голос.

Ответа нет! Отвергнул струны я,
Да хрящ другой мне будет плодоносен!
И вот ему несет рука моя
Зародыши елей, дубов и сосен.

ON PLANTING A WOOD

Spring's here again; again the meadows laugh,
the wood rejoices in its girlish green,
the indefatigable farmer's plough
again in humble hope furrows the fields.

But spring no longer sets my soul alight,
and hope no longer charms my weary way,
the world is already slipping from my sight,
my eyelids sinking before eternal day.

My head is already silvered by the winter
that warms the seed-corn for a future life,
but the bard has not yet crossed the fatal frontier –
his lyre can still be heard by those on earth.

Great is the Lord! compassionate, but just:
nothing that happens here escapes his sight;
He can forgive our follies, but not the feasts
where evil words are born of evil thought.

If someone was wounded by my hasty words,
he could have clashed with me in open battle;
but they dug a hidden trap deep in the woods
and decked their horns with my reputation's tatters.

My soul reached out to embrace new generations,
I loved, I cherished their still barren fields,
I tried in vain to wake the hearts of mortals
and teach them how to speak the good we feel.

No answer! I have thrown away my lyre –
let a fresh patch of ground bear better fruit!
I carry in my hands the nursery
from which great oaks and pines and firs will shoot.

И пусть! Простяся с лирою моей,
Я верую: ее заменят эти,
Поэзии таинственных скорбей
Могучие и сумрачные дети.

So may it be! Setting my strings aside,
I put my faith instead in these young trees,
mighty and twilight beings, each a child
of the mysterious griefs of poetry.

ПИРОСКАФ

Дикою, грозною ласкою полны,
Бьют в наш корабль средиземные волны.
Вот над кормою стал капитан.
Визгнул свисток его. Братствуя с паром,
Ветру наш парус раздался недаром:
Пенясь, глубоко вздохнул океан!

Мчимся. Колеса могучей машины
Роют волнистое лоно пучины.
Парус надулся. Берег исчез.
Наедине мы с морскими волнами,
Только что чайка вьется за нами
Белая, рея меж вод и небес.

Только вдали, океана жилица,
Чайке подобна, вод его птица,
Парус развив, как большое крыло,
С бурной стихией в томительном споре,
Лодка рыбачья качается в море, –
С брегом набрежное скрылось, ушло!

Много земель я оставил за мною;
Вынес я много смятенной душою
Радостей ложных, истинных зол;
Много мятежных решил я вопросов,
Прежде чем руки марсельских матросов
Подняли якорь, надежды символ!

С детства влекла меня сердца тренога
В область свободную влажного бога;
Жадные длани я к ней простирал,
Темную страсть мою днесь награждая,
Кротко щадит меня немочь морская:
Пеною здравья брызжет мне вал!

STEAMSHIP

Swollen with savage, terrible affection,
they batter us, the Mediterranean waves.
Then high above our stern we see the captain.
A blast from his whistle, and suddenly our sail
flings open to the wind, joins hands with steam:
ocean's deep sighing scatters into foam.

We hurtle on. The mighty engine's wheels
tear at the billowing bosom of the deep.
The sail swells out. The shore has disappeared.
We are alone among the warring waves;
only a seagull circling in our wake
skims white between the water and the sky.

Only, far off, a dweller of the seas,
bird of the waves, a sister of the gull,
spreading its sail like a wide-stretching wing,
wearily struggling in the turbulent flow,
a fishing boat is rocking on the ocean –
both land and shoreline are clean gone from vision.

I have left many countries in my wake;
my soul, confused by contrary directions,
has suffered both false joys and genuine woes;
I had confronted many perplexing questions
before the sailors of Marseille hauled up
the anchor, emblem of a new-found hope.

From childhood my tumultuous heart has carried me
over the free realms of the watery god;
I greedily stretched out my hands to it.
And as a reward for my dark passion here
the sea's distemper gently strokes my head,
the breakers splash me with the foam of health.

Нужды нет, близко ль, далеко ль до брега!
В сердце к нему приготовлена нега.
Вижу Фетиду; мне жребий благой
Емлет она из лазоревой урны:
Завтра увижу я башни Ливурны,
Завтра увижу Элизий земной!

What does it matter if the shore is far or near!
The heart already warms to its delight.
I gaze on Thetis, she draws out for me
a happy destiny from her azure urn.
Tomorrow I see the towers of Leghorn.
Tomorrow I see Elysium on earth!

YEVGENY BARATYNSKY was born in 1840 to a gentry family in the Tambov region of central Russia. He was educated at the elite St. Petersburg School of Pages, but was expelled for his part in a youthful robbery. After a spell of suicidal depression, he enlisted as a soldier and served for some years in Finland. During this period, he wrote many poems; he is now recognized (together with Pushkin and others) as a member of the gifted 'Pléiade' of Russia's Golden Age. In 1825 he was pardoned and promoted to officer rank, whereupon he retired, married Nastasya Engelgardt and settled in the country near Moscow. There he lived a happily married and outwardly uneventful life, publishing poetic collections in 1827 and 1835, followed by his masterpiece *Half-light* in 1842. The following year he made his first visit to western Europe, spending a winter in Paris, then moving to Naples, where he died unexpectedly in 1844.

PETER FRANCE was born in Northern Ireland of Welsh parents and has lived at various places in England, France and Canada. He is now based in Edinburgh, where he was professor of French from 1980 to 2000. He has written many studies of French and Russian literature (including *Poets of Modern Russia*, 1982), and is the editor of the *Oxford Guide to Literature in English Translation* and general editor of the five-volume Oxford *History of Literary Translation in English*. He has translated French and Russian prose texts as well as several volumes of Russian poetry – Blok and Pasternak (both with Jon Stallworthy), Mayakovsky, Lermontov, Mandelstam, and in particular Gennady Aygi. He is married to the historian and translator Siân Reynolds.

ROGNVALDR KALI KOLSSON, EARL OF ORKNEY
Crimsoning the Eagle's Claw
Selected, translated from the Old Norse
and introduced by Ian Crockatt
with a Preface by Kevin-Crossley Holland

CHARLES BAUDELAIRE
Selected Poems from 'Les Fleurs du Mal'
Translated from the French by Jan Owen
and introduced by Rosemary Lloyd

ED. PHILIP WILSON
The Bright Rose
EARLY GERMAN VERSE 800-1280
Selected, translated from the Old High
and Middle High German
and introduced by Philip Wilson

Further titles of poetry in translation are available in
'Arc Visible Poets', 'Arc Translations', 'Arc Anthologies' and
'New Voices from Europe & Beyond' (anthologies)

www.arcpublications.co.uk